Scene 1

MUM	Pandora, I'm going out to the shop now. I'll be back in a minute. Be a good girl and do your homework. And remember what I said.
PANDORA	I know. Don't go out.
MUM	And don't let anyone in.
PANDORA	Not even my friends. It's not fair.
MUM	Yes it is, Pandora. They made a terrible mess last time. Now do your homework and keep the house tidy. And don't . . .
PANDORA	. . . sit watching television. I know!
MUM	Bye, Pandora!

(Mum goes out.)

3

PANDORA   Bye, Mum!
Do this! Don't do that!
I'm going to do what I want.
I don't want to do homework.
I'm going to watch telly.
What's on?

(She switches on the television.)

PANDORA   Oh good, pirates. I like pirates.
They're on their ship, *The
Saucy Sausage.*
That's Pirate Bogey-Beard.
He looks fierce.
And that's Captain Very-Cross Bones.
He looks fiercer. And that's Tim,
the cabin-boy.
Oh! Poor Tim. The pirates are
making him walk the plank.

4

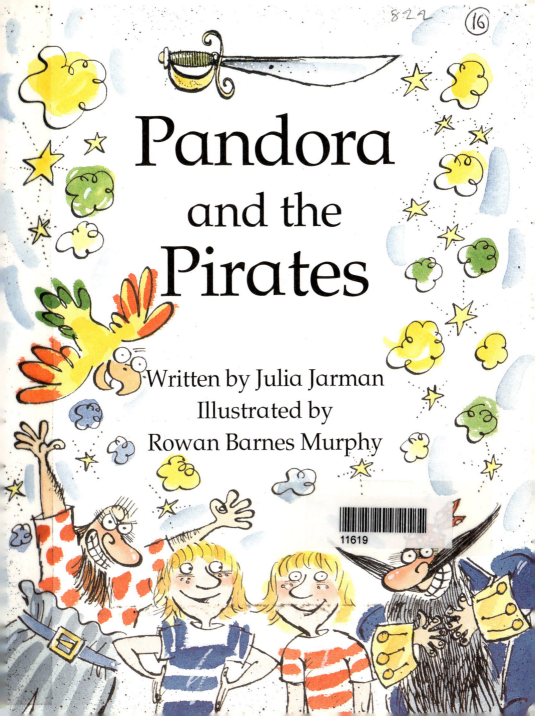

Pandora
and the
Pirates

Written by Julia Jarman
Illustrated by
Rowan Barnes Murphy

Scene 2

PIRATE BOGEY-BEARD
Walk the plank!

CAPTAIN VERY-CROSS BONES
Walk the plank, boy!

PARROT   Walk! Walk!
Squawk! Squawk!

PIRATES   Shut up, Parrot.

TIM   No! No! I don't want to
walk the plank!
Look at those sharks!

PIRATE BOGEY-BEARD
You put barnacles in
our bedsocks.

PARROT   Bedsocks. Dead socks.

PIRATES   Shut up, Parrot.

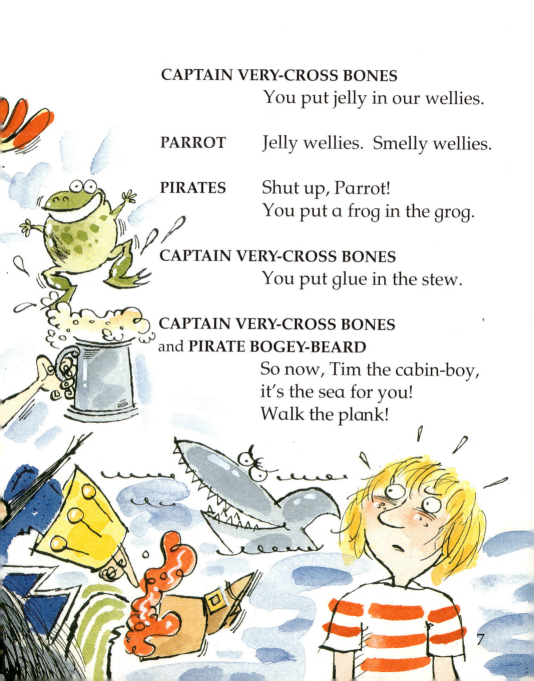

CAPTAIN VERY-CROSS BONES
You put jelly in our wellies.

PARROT   Jelly wellies. Smelly wellies.

PIRATES   Shut up, Parrot!
You put a frog in the grog.

CAPTAIN VERY-CROSS BONES
You put glue in the stew.

CAPTAIN VERY-CROSS BONES
and **PIRATE BOGEY-BEARD**
So now, Tim the cabin-boy,
it's the sea for you!
Walk the plank!

7

TIM   No! No!

CAPTAIN VERY-CROSS BONES
and **PIRATE BOGEY-BEARD**
        Yes! Yes!
        (They push Tim.)

TIM   No! Oh!
        (Tim bounces off the other end.)

PANDORA Oh no! He's jumped out of the telly.
(Tim the cabin-boy lands on the sitting-room carpet, in front of Pandora.)
My mum won't like this.

Scene 3

TIM   Don't just stand there!
Hide me! Quick!
Those two pirates want to kill me!

PANDORA   Sorry. My mum said I can't have
anyone in.
You must go back.

TIM   I can't, Pandora!
Look at those two!
Listen to them.
        (He points at the pirates.)

PIRATE BOGEY-BEARD

Where's he gone?
Where's the boy gone?

CAPTAIN VERY-CROSS BONES

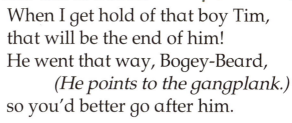

When I get hold of that boy Tim,
that will be the end of him!
He went that way, Bogey-Beard,
(He points to the gangplank.)
so you'd better go after him.

PIRATE BOGEY-BEARD

I'm not walking the plank.

CAPTAIN VERY-CROSS BONES

Yes, you are!
*(He pushes Pirate Bogey-Beard
along the gangplank.)*

PIRATE BOGEY-BEARD

No! No! No!
*(Then Pirate Bogey-Beard
bounces off the other end.)*

11

Scene 4

PIRATE BOGEY-BEARD
Oh Oh Oh!

PANDORA Oh no! Here's a pirate!
And a parrot!
They've jumped out of the telly too.
Hide in the kitchen, Tim –
but my mum won't like this at all.
*(She opens the door and
Tim goes into the kitchen.)*

PIRATE BOGEY-BEARD

Now where's that cabin-boy?
(He looks around and
sees Pandora.)
Ah there you are!
(He grabs her.)
Got you, Tim!

PANDORA   I'm not Tim!

PIRATE BOGEY-BEARD

Yes you are.
You're Tim the cabin-boy and
you're coming back to *The Saucy*
Sausage.

PANDORA   I'm not!
(She gets away and goes
behind the sofa.)

PIRATE BOGEY-BEARD
        You are!

PANDORA   I'm not! I'm not Tim the cabin-boy
        and I can't come back with you.
        So there! My mum said I can't.

PIRATE BOGEY-BEARD
        What's your mum got to do with it?

PANDORA   She said I can't go out
        and I can't have my friends in
        – because they make a mess.
        Look at all this.
            (She points to the mess.)

PIRATE BOGEY-BEARD

But I'm not your friend, am I?
I'm Pirate Bogey-Beard,
the fiercest, gruesomest pirate
that ever sailed the stormy seas.

CAPTAIN VERY-CROSS BONES

Oh no you're not!
I'M the fiercest, gruesomest pirate
that ever sailed the stormy seas.
Now stop talking and get back
here with him!

PANDORA   NO!
If I go off with you two, my mum
will kill me.

CAPTAIN VERY-CROSS BONES
> Oh, don't worry about that,
> Tim boy.

PANDORA   Why not?

CAPTAIN VERY-CROSS BONES
> Because I'll kill you first!
> Come here, you!
> > *(He steps out of the television
> > and grabs her.)*

PIRATE BOGEY-BEARD

> Oh no you don't! I'm the fiercest
> and I'll kill her first!
> *(He grabs Pandora.)*

CAPTAIN VERY-CROSS BONES

> No you won't! I will!
> *(He grabs Pandora.)*
> I'm the fiercest, gruesomest pirate
> that ever sailed the stormy sea,
> and if you say I'm not, I'll slash you.
> *(He slashes the air with his
> cutlass and Pandora gets away.)*

PANDORA Great! While you two pirates fight,
> I'm getting out of sight.
> *(Pandora hides.)*

PIRATE BOGEY-BEARD

> I'm the fiercest, gruesomest pirate
> that ever sailed the stormy sea,
> and if you say I'm not, I'll bash you.

17

PANDORA   These two pirates are very dim.
             See me trick both him and him.
                    (She hides behind Pirate Bogey-
                    Beard.)
             I'll make my voice sound like
             Pirate Bogey-Beard's.

> I'm the fiercest gruesomest
> pirate that ever sailed the
> stormy sea and if you say
> I'm not, Cross Bones,
> I'll pull your moustache !

CAPTAIN VERY-CROSS BONES
             You wouldn't dare!

PIRATE BOGEY-BEARD
             What?

CAPTAIN VERY-CROSS BONES
             Pull my moustache!

PIRATE BOGEY-BEARD
             If you say so.
                    (He pulls Captain-Very Cross
                    Bones's moustache. It comes off.)

CAPTAIN VERY-CROSS BONES
> OUCH!
> Now you're for it.
> I'm going to bash you and slash you.

PARROT Bash! Slash!

PIRATE BOGEY-BEARD
> And I'm going to slash you and
> bash you!
> > *(The pirates fight.)*

PARROT Bash! Slash!

PANDORA Fight away, fight away, you two.
I've got a lot of tidying up to do.

Scene 5

PANDORA I must tidy up before my mum gets back.
(She starts to tidy up.)

PARROT Bash! Crash!
Look out! Look out!
The pirates have knocked each other out.
One! Two! Three! Four! . . .

PANDORA *(She sees her mum through the window.)*
Help! My mum is at the door.

PARROT   Five, six, seven, eight . . .

PANDORA   Help me tidy up, parrot!

PARROT   It's too late.
                (Pandora's mum comes into the sitting-room.)

MUM   Pandora! Look at this mess.
                What are these pirates doing on my floor?
                I said keep the house tidy, don't have
                your friends in, and don't watch
                television.

MUM That TV can go off for a start.
(She turns the television off.
The pirates and the parrot
vanish into the television.)
Good, those pirates have gone.
I'll get a brush.
(She goes into the kitchen.)

PANDORA Bye, parrot. Bye, pirates.
But what about Tim? Did he go too?
I want the telly on, Mum!
(She turns the television on.)
Oh, now it's the Oat Pops advert.

MUM *(Mum comes in, with Tim.)*
I said OFF, Pandora.
And who's this boy? I found him in
the kitchen.

PANDORA It's Tim!
Tim!

MUM Pandora, I said no friends and
no television!
*(Mum switches off the
television. Tim flies into it.)*

PANDORA Oh no!

MUM Oh yes! And now they've all gone
I'll get the vacuum cleaner.
You can start tidying.
(She opens the kitchen door.)

PANDORA Okay, but first I want to see where Tim is.
(She switches on the television again.)
Great.   There he is, eating Oat Pops. Happy at last! Bye, Tim.